AMERICAN TOW TRUCKS

The Custom Wrecker Scene in the USA

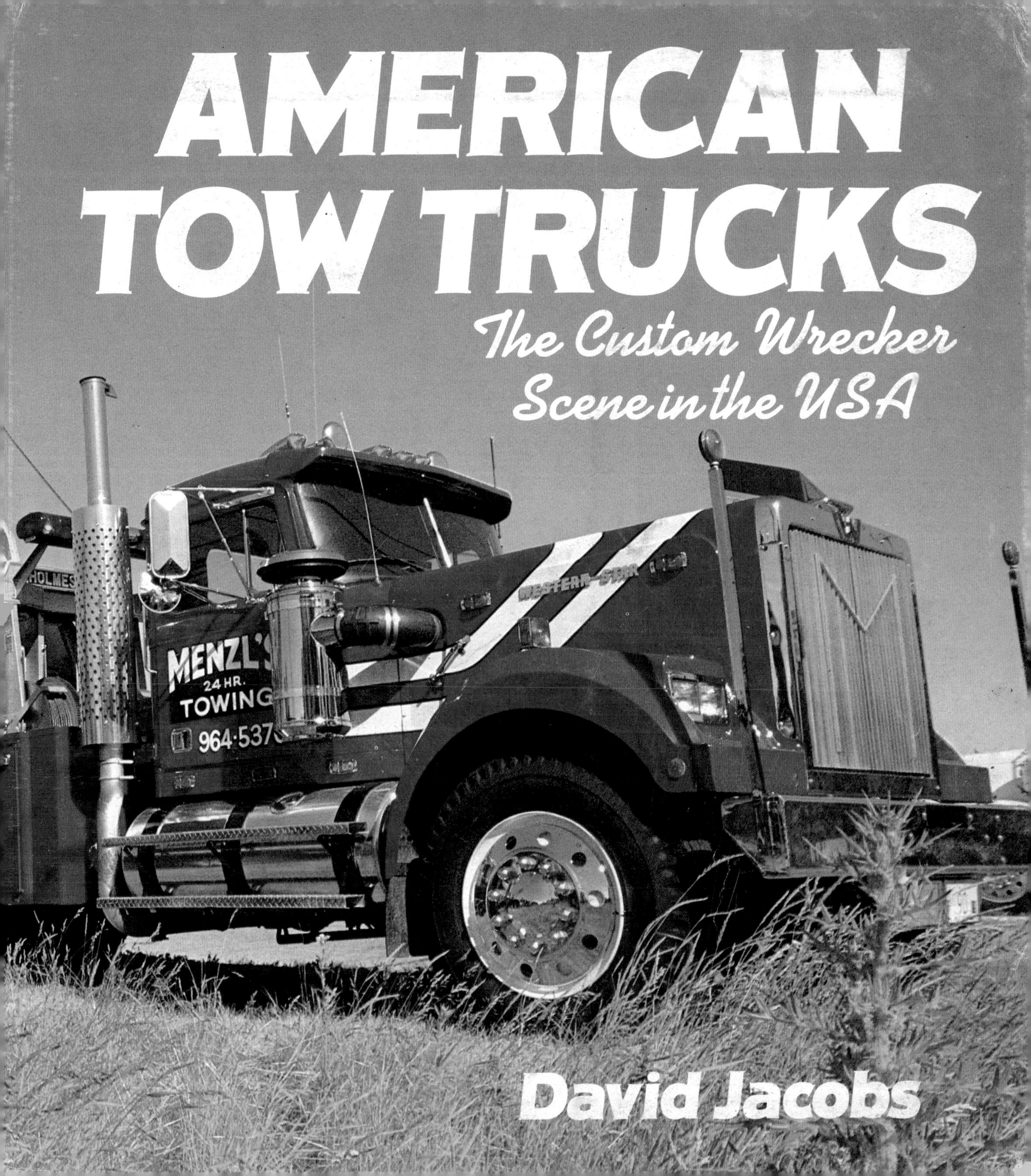

David Jacobs

Published in 1986 by Osprey Publishing Limited
12–14 Long Acre, London WC2E 9LP
Member company of the George Philip Group

British Library Cataloguing in Publication Data
Jacobs, David, *1952*–
    American Tow Trucks.—(Osprey colour series)
    1. Wreckers (Vehicles)
    I. Title
    629.2'25   TL230.5.W/
ISBN 0–85045–692–4

Printed in Italy

Contents

Introduction

Straps and winches, booms and lifts, are all part of the tow truck jargon. All the trucks shown in this latest addition to the Osprey Colour Series are working trucks, each earning a decent living for their respective owner/driver. Without the tow truck or wrecker, American highways would become a chaotic nightmare of broken-down cars and trucks, not to mention crashed and neglected vehicles. *American Tow Trucks* shows you that the American trucker handles his rig with pride and enthusiasm, even under the worst conditions. In *American Tow Trucks* we also visit the ever-popular tow shows, in which drivers and enthusiasts alike can enjoy many diverse activities, including truck beauty contests and displays of driving skills, and also trade stands and show trucks.

David Jacobs gives us tow trucks at work and play, but above all what comes across is their aesthetic beauty. This is true at all times and in the dirtiest situations, but is shown to perfection in the shots from the shows at La Crosse and New Orleans.

David Jacobs likes to be known as a semi-professional photographer for he has had several books published of nothing but his photographs as well as posters, shots in brochures and magazines. Full time, however, he accepts he runs a communications business in London specializing in graphics, 'instant printing', computer typesetting and photography. He uses mainly Nikon equipment with Kodak film. For those photography enthusiasts who enjoy seeing strong blue skies, David recommends a polarizing filter which he always has fitted to his Nikon 20 and 28 mm lenses.

David's books, all published by Osprey Publishing, are as follows: AMERICAN TRUCKS, AMERICAN TRUCKS 2, CUSTOM & RACE TRUCKS, EUROPEAN TRUCKS, AMERICAN BUSES and now AMERICAN TOW TRUCKS.

David's fascination with America and Americana continues apace. He makes regular visits from England to fill his photographic library.

David would once again like to thank his many trucking friends who have tolerated his fanaticism, and apologies for any friendships he might have wrecked along the way!

Thanks then to Towing and Recovery Association of America, especially Michael and Randee McGovern, John Hawkins of Tow Times, Wreckers International, The Wisconsin Towing Association, Kelly McKnight Wrecker Services of Arlington, Texas, Michael Bigg's Towing Company, Newburgh, New York. Thanks also to Ash, Denise, Scott and Suzanne, Andy, Judy, Vanessa, Viv, Nat, Leslie, Naomi, Daniel, John, Dick and Jill, Linda, Ruth, Karen, Jeff, Sharon, Mary-Ann, Debbs, John and Mary.

The tow truck at work

Left Garbage truck out of New Orleans looking for a tow. Bob Kingsmill, of Kingsmill's Auto Services LA, keeps his 'pants' oil free by laying down the 'magic' carpet

Below Target in sight. The truck's in a tangle, or is that a triangle!

A Mack conventional
wrecker lifts an
International cabover under
a blazing Texan sky

Above The ops room at Kelly McKnight's – closed-circuit TV monitors the storage yard. This is one of the country's largest tow companies: maps, videos and telephone taping of messages ensure accurate recording of incident details

Left What's cooking?

A new slant on home removals. An Allied
Van Lines International truck is salvaged
by Kelly McKnight

This was an easy one for
Kelly McKnight's wrecker –
next call might be a plane
in a swamp

A distinctive red and yellow Mack
conventional ready to go

Above Keeping fit trucker-style

Overleaf Immaculate Holmes 750 wrecker lifts a beaten-up Ford conventional

17

The end of the story – parking the
International

Discussing an engine refit at Michael Bigg's. Men of all work, drivers are also mechanics, painters, and fabricators

Left One of the best

Right Keeping in touch – the mast has a range of 100 miles

Below A lowboy in a tight corner. Michael Bigg's amazing towing company boasts six heavy-duty trucks. All are kept immaculately clean, washed and dried after every job

Previous page The police and five Michael Bigg trucks home in on a rolled over cement mixer. This is a 'routine' job for this family-run firm based at Vail's Gate, Newburgh, New York. The Bigg's outfit wins many prizes and awards at tow shows throughout the US

Left What to do next – lifting the mixer on to a hydraulic lowboy

Below Sparkling chrome on a working 1985 Freightliner. Note the rectangular headlamp

All in a day's work – using the Freightliner to winch the mixer off the lowboy

Below Rock hard cement?

Right The downside of trucking: chains like these could take your arms off. These will secure the International to the heavy duty hydraulic arms of the wrecker

Left A reefer in the sand out of New Orleans. A 1972 Autocar with a 1982 Century 40-ton wrecker

Below You've seen this one before. The reefer back on the road. The ground is very soft in this part of New Orleans, so this 'sinking feeling' is common

Small is beautiful. Note the safety straps
on this Century telescopic lifting bar

Towing folk

Above Kelly McKnight mark 2, complete with stetson

Left Starting out. Note Motorola communications system

This is Dallas country

No mistaking this police reserve's message
at the La Crosse tow show in Wisconsin

Above Heavy-duty trucking is not for the boys. Robert Seeman's left arm was severed by a snapped chain

Left This Dragon Wagon has real fire. The truckers' gear is standard

Left Driver comfort is everything. Note the air ride seat

Below Day for night in Wisconsin

Even the top men get involved in the show
– one of the Bertagnolli brothers at work.
The 1984 Peterbilt conventional has TV,
fridge and air conditioning – yours for
$185,000

Gleaming Boss Hogg. Our stetson clad trucker fits a 'light' antennae to this white road boss conventional

Nice colour co-ordinated
Kenworth conventional.
Note TRAA (Towing and
Recovery Association of
America) symbol on
trucker's shirt

Novel transport at La Crosse. Discussing
the day's events perhaps

Left Did you hear me?

Above What's going on up top?

Convention time – wreckers at play

The grand finale – convoy out of La Crosse over the Mississippi. At this well organized show more than one hundred beautiful trucks parade around town

This eye-catching candy-apple red beauty
has independent front and rear steering.
It's a 1979 Ford 1-ton with a Challenger
single line hydraulic. A 600 horse-power
engine fires this superb 'show and go'
wrecker

A room with a view. The La Crosse tow
show from a Kenworth Aerodyne sleeping
compartment, 15 feet off the ground

Bert's Peterbilt sparkles in the midday sun
outside the New Orleans superdome

Going to the show in style

Superb paintwork detail on this black beauty. A Gimmie with a Holmes wrecker

Below Whiter than white, except it's an Autocar!

Right Me and my shadow. Note castors on hydraulic lift

Right Backing-up against the clock

Below Matchless chrome

Above Party time in Wisconsin

Left Big boom   **Below** No flies on this one

A classic Mack. This 1959 B73 has 200,000
miles on the clock

Outstanding Gimmie conventional. Note
duo-tone paintwork

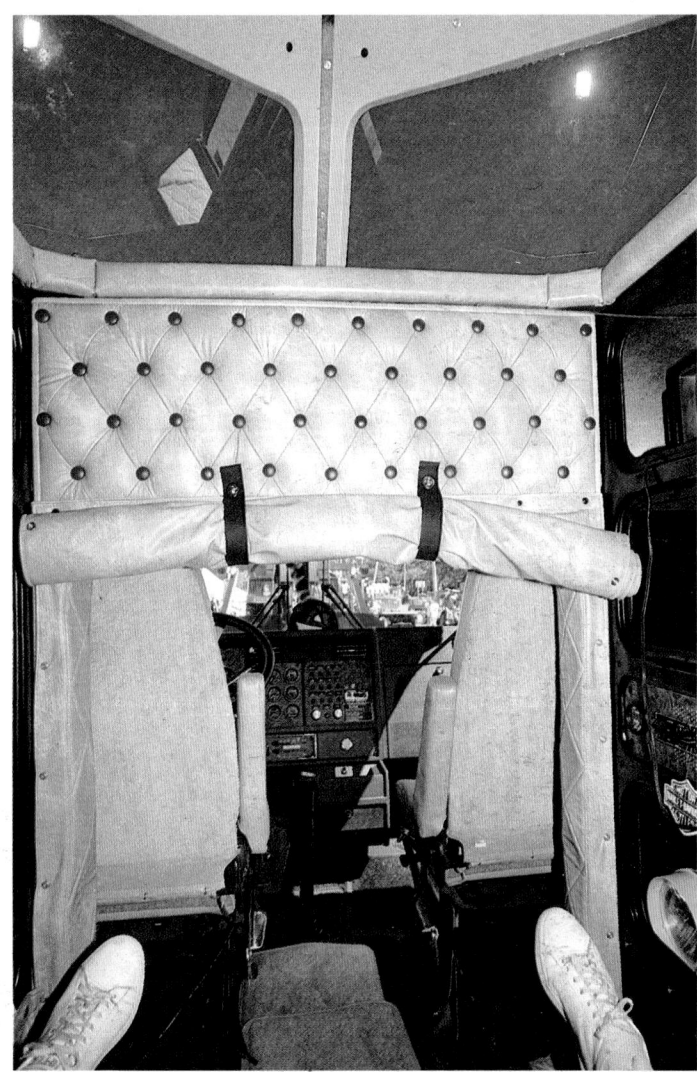

Above David Jacobs puts his feet in it. Diamond-studded upholstery in a Kenworth King-size Aerodyne sleeper

Left Holiday Kenworth conventional waits in line to be judged at La Crosse

No tangling with the nudge bar on this
unusual International Paystar 5000

Not even the chrome outshines the
paintwork on the Aerodyne Kenworth

Prize-winning Challenger wrecker fitted to a conventional Peterbilt truck. Western star conventional behind. Kevin Cleary runs these amazing wreckers out of Suffern, New York. Both are kept spotless and ready to roll 24 hours a day. Kevin has won many awards with the Peterbilt and keeps it in an atmospherically pure garage. But it's on hand for all emergencies

Night owl

As first seen in *Custom and Race Trucks* –
at speed

Holiday truck at the
Holiday Inn – hydraulic
lowboy on the back of a
stunning Kenworth cabover

Big Tow again – which way to turn?

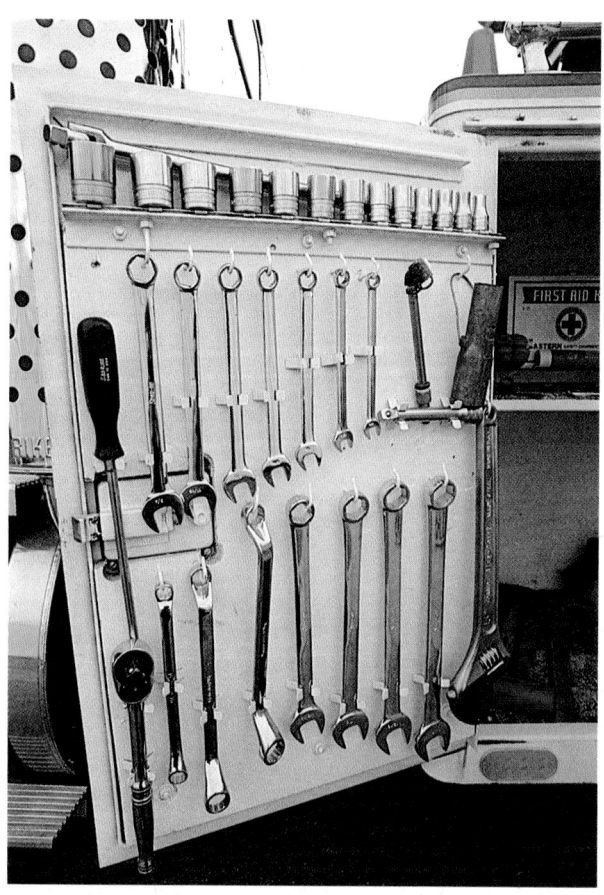

Above Toolkit

Above right Beat this. There's no place like Holmes

Right Reach for the sky. Boom length, more than 100 ft

Metallic green and gold
paintwork on an
immaculate Autocar
conventional

Showtime under the dome

A husband-and-wife team run this neat 1973 Chevy C50 with a Holmes 480 8-ton wrecker

Randy's — a rebuilt cargo van with a moon roof and cruise control. Note VIP customer suite

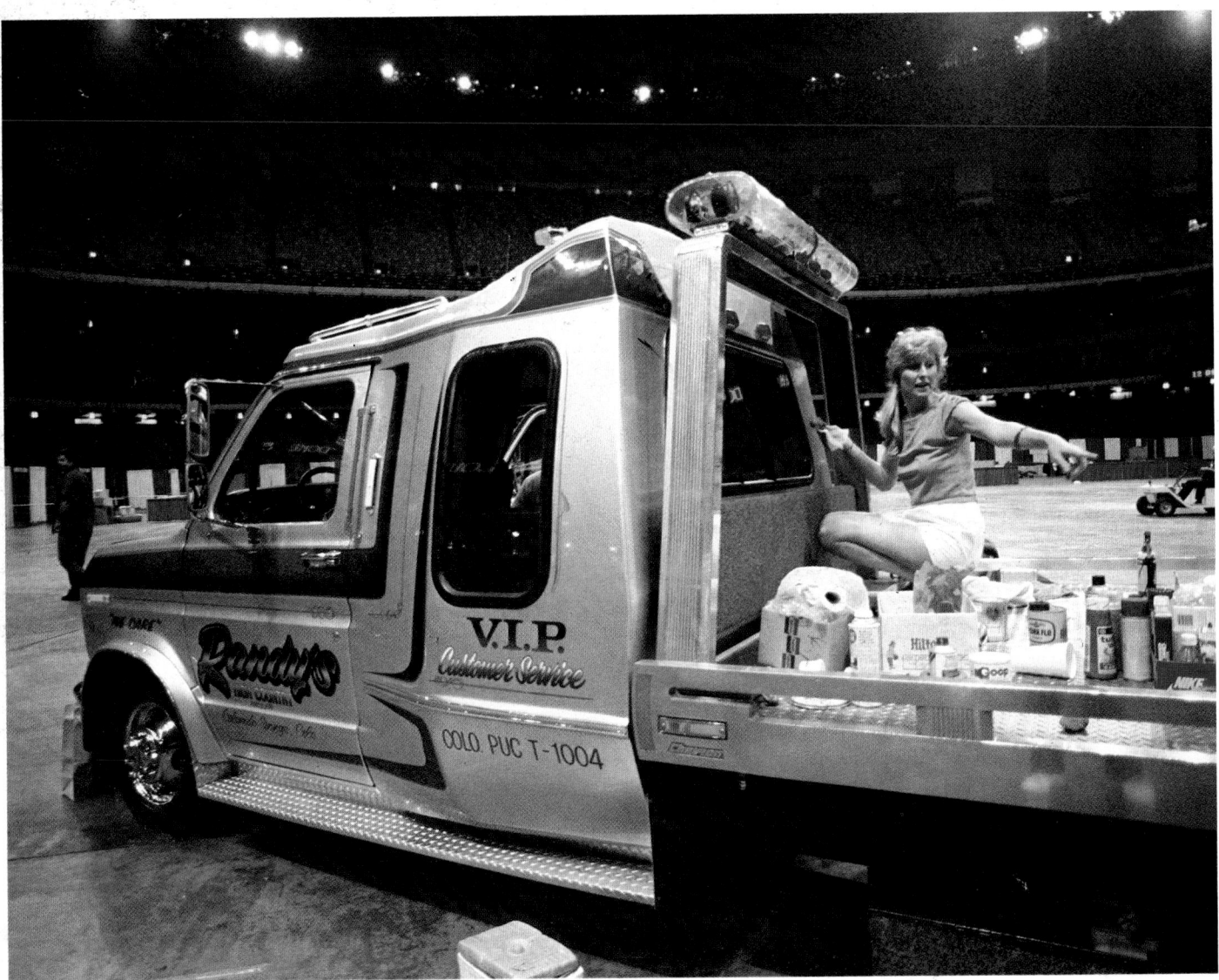

This tasteful cream and brown outfit has
10-speed Eaton transmission and a
Challenger 8800 40-ton wrecker

Left The heavy-duty brigade on parade **Below** Lighting umbrellas highlight the star

Fun paintwork on a classic
Mack

Left Hold it right there! Note chrome seats – to a panning camera they will look like real people

Below The quick way off a lowboy

Left Basking in the applause – a gleaming International

Below What's going on in there?

Praise the Lord – this 1974
Peterbilt has that extra
protection

Getting the show on the road in New
Orleans

Yellow carpet treatment

Left Even booms are cut down to size in the biggest dome on Earth

Below Neat for the street

Above Classy black pickup

Left In a dome this size radio communication is a must. This white-clad marshal carries a two-way radio for instant answers

The Western flavour

On the launching pad

Right Night lights

Below Sunset glow on a Chevy Silverado

Careful detailing on Bambarger's 1967
International with a Holmes 16-ton
wrecker

Riding in style – a Chevy carrying a
Chevy?

Berts lights up at the Bud Light sign

Custom wrecker paint

Not short on style

Fit for a King

Class glass

Keeping the name clean

Airbrushed glory

Kenworth Automatic – conventionally good

Two ways of looking at it

No mistaking this one

Reflections

Who'd take this on?

Bert's a lucky man

Bigg's boom